RALEIGH

A CLOSER LOOK: GLOBAL INDUSTRIES

FASHION INDUSTRY

ROSIE WILSON

rosen publishing's
rosen central

New York

Published in 2011 by The Rosen Publishing Group Inc.
29 East 21st Street, New York, NY 10010

Copyright © 2011 Wayland/The Rosen Publishing Group, Inc.

Series Editor: Claire Shanahan
Editor: Susie Brooks
Consultant: Steph Warren
Designer: Rebecca Painter
Picture Researcher: Shelley Noronha

First Edition

Library of Congress Cataloging-in-Publication Data

Wilson, Rosie.
 Fashion industry / Rosie Wilson. — 1st ed.
    p. cm. — (A closer look: Global industries)
 Includes index.
 ISBN 978-1-4358-9631-4 (library binding)
 ISBN 978-1-4358-9637-6 (paperback)
 ISBN 978-1-4358-9643-7 (6-pack)
 1. Fashion merchandising—Juvenile literature. 2. Clothing
trade—Juvenile literature. I. Title.
 HD9940.A2W56 2010
 338.4'774692—dc22
                                              2009047311

Photographs
6, 8, 9, 10, 15, 17, 18, 19, 27 EASI-Images/Rob Bowden; 13, 20,
32, 34, 36 Getty Images; 21 © KIN HEUNG/Reuters/Corbis; 22
credit: Topfoto; 28 © Frank Miller/Corbis; 30 EASI-Images/Roy
Maconachie; 33 © WWD/Condé Nast/Corbis; 35 © MIKE CASSESE/
Reuters/ Corbis; 38 Joerg Boethling/Alamy; 40 People Tree

Manufactured in Malaysia
CPSIA Compliance Information: Batch #WAS0102YA: For Further Information
Contact Rosen Publishing, New York, New York at 1-800-237-9932

Contents

The World is Our Wardrobe!

Emily gets into her new clothes, ready for school. Today is a nonuniform day, but she needs her sports bag, too. She'll wear gym shoes anyway—the newest design, which cost five times as much as the rest of her outfit. Her T-shirt was a bargain from the store nearby and it looks just like one worn by a celebrity in Emily's favorite magazine. Emily never looks at labels on the inside, but if she did, she would find that the T-shirt came from the Dominican Republic, the jeans from Tunisia, and the gym shoes from China. Her jewelry— another bargain—was made in India. None of the workers who made Emily's clothes were paid enough to live, but she doesn't know this.

Going Global

Global industries work across nations and continents, producing and selling in several countries, and affecting the lives of people around the world. The fashion industry involves everyone who makes, sources, or sells products (clothes, accessories, coats, and shoes) for customers to wear. It also includes the producers of raw materials such as cotton, metals, rubber, and wool. Sometimes the clothing industry is called the garment or apparel industry. The global fashion industry has several centers of production, where clothes are made, and other centers of retail, where they are sold.

Young people enjoy shopping in Harajuku, a district of Tokyo, Japan. Fashion styles vary widely, even within a single street.

Globalization: a Shrinking World

Globalization means that we live in a smaller, more connected, more interdependent world. Physically, the world is not smaller, but it feels smaller because we have access to more of it. Geographical distances seem nearer because it takes less time now to travel to them or communicate between them. This has been made possible by improvements in technology. Cell phones, the internet, low-cost flights, and cheaper cars are all examples of this. Global connections are faster, easier, and cheaper, which means that industries use them more. It can be easy for those living in more developed countries (MDCs) to take this for granted, but the technological revolution has not taken place at the same rate all over the world. As a result, some countries have benefited more than others from globalization.

Winners and Losers

The global fashion industry has both winners and losers. Powerful global companies make large profits and provide their customers in MDCs with a wide range of products at low prices. Less developed countries (LDCs) such as China, Turkey, and Bangladesh provide labor and benefit from the industry, with new roads, schools, and hospitals being built.

However, many individuals in LDCs work long hours in factories making fashion products, and do not earn a living wage (enough money daily to feed their family and provide shelter). Poverty levels remain high in these places, while many people in the United States, the United Kingdom (UK), and Japan, for instance, have more than they need and can afford to buy a new fashion item every week. There are losers in MDCs, too, as fashion companies buy from factories and contractors all across the world, so local manufacturers have closed down due to competition.

> *I am angry because of what is happening to these workers, who sew the clothes we wear... We need to expose the corporations that are growing ever richer off the backs of workers trapped in appalling conditions in the developing world.*

Anita Roddick, *The Economist*, July/August 2004

A Fashion World

Fashion is a global industry because it affects everyone in the world. Clothing is a basic need to keep us warm and protect our bodies, but today, clothing also sends messages about what kind of person the wearer is. Billions of dollars are involved in making, transporting, and selling clothing, accessories, and shoes. Some people spend much of their income on "high fashion" items, trendy because they were bought extremely recently. In the UK, over the period 1996–2005, 2.2 million tons of clothing and textiles were consumed per year, at a value of $72 billion. Many people worldwide are involved in this process at different stages. After first use, the things we wear often start another journey—to charity shops, the trash, or sometimes to be resold far across the globe.

Most fashion products travel many miles around the world before reaching the consumer. Many are transported in shipping containers like these.

Fashion Connections

Fashion has a history of global connections and has played an important role in the rise of global trade and globalization. The Silk Road from India to Europe brought cloths and gems as early as the fourth century, but the route was difficult and dangerous. Ships exploring the oceans to find a faster, easier route discovered the American continent and Africa, and eventually circumnavigated the globe. Cotton, too, has a global history, and the trade triangle (including cotton) that developed between Europe, North and South America, and Africa fueled the Transatlantic Slave Trade (see page 24). The desire for precious stones and gold is present in many cultures, and such treasures have often been traded for other products or used as symbols of wealth, royalty, and power.

Shoppers stroll around the Queen Victoria Building shopping mall in Sydney, Australia. The mall has over 200 stores, many of them selling global brands, and is also a popular place to eat, meet friends, and relax.

SPOTLIGHT

Why Has the Global Fashion Industry Grown?

Global Trends

Trends and styles spread across the globe in various ways. They are publicized through the global media (movies, magazines, etc.), and through transnational companies (TNCs) who sell the same products in many countries. Patterns of employment have boosted spending, too, since most people work in services (shops, offices, hospitals, schools, etc.) in many countries. These types of job often require people to look smart, even attractive. It is not acceptable in some careers to be "out-of-fashion."

Shopping Habits

The purpose of shopping has changed from buying basic essentials to being a leisure activity. Purchasing products has also become a sign of wealth and status—for example, a BMW or a Chanel shopping bag mean the same thing in Beijing, Nairobi, London, and Rio. Consumption is part of our global culture now, and a way to relax or spend time with others. Shopping centers also provide leisure facilities such as movie theaters and restaurants. However, during times of economic hardship, there is usually a fall in consumption, causing problems for many fashion retailers, and raising questions about the future of the industry.

Technology

The technology and machinery that make fashion items enable global production to work. Factories can mass-produce, and transportation costs are low per item when quantities are high, so it is worth sourcing materials and labor from around the world. Fabric is woven and spun easily using large machines, and shoes can be mass-produced, too. Jewelry parts are often cast or molded using machinery and power tools, in contrast to the laborious handcrafting of the past.

Fashion Locations

Many countries in the world used to have their own garment industry. Now, different stages of the process are located in different places, including rural areas, industrial sites, distribution centers, and retail stores (in cities and their surrounds). Globalization has led to garments being made, finished, and labeled in several different countries before reaching their final destination. Newly built shopping areas are the most popular, therefore, city centers need to regularly change in order to attract consumers. Online shopping is becoming more widely used. Although market stalls are no longer a regular source for fashion items in MDCs, they still play a major role in LDCs, and discarded clothes are also exported to these markets to be resold.

Market sellers in Jinja, Uganda, arrange clothing to be sold. After first use, many fashion items are exported to secondhand markets in LDCs.

Rising Economies

Fast-developing nations play their own part in shaping the fashion industry. For example, in India, due to a flourishing economy, some people have more money to spend on consumer goods including clothing and fashion accessories, shoes, and watches. India was the 12th-richest nation in the world in 2007. However, although $36 billion was spent in India on clothing and fashion accessories in 2007, around 80 percent of the country's population live on $2 a day or less. The majority, therefore, have little access to the fashion industry, highlighting the imbalance in wealth that is typical of many nations, especially those developing fast.

SPOTLIGHT

Export Processing Zones

Export processing zones (EPZs) are areas set up within a country to attract foreign investors, often to produce goods to be sold abroad. Fashion factories that locate themselves in an EPZ can benefit from the cheaper labor of that country and also from lower or no taxes. LDCs use these zones to develop industry and provide jobs, but there are many cases where labor laws and human rights have been violated in EPZ workplaces, and the laws surrounding these areas are often unclear. Sometimes these zones can be industry-specific—there is a jewelry zone in Thailand and a leather zone in Turkey, for instance. In China, there are several special economic zones, which are similar to EPZs.

Time for Change?

Some experts say that consumers are becoming concerned about inequality in the fashion industry. Ethical clothing, accessories, and footwear are now popular, and are even offered by some mainstream companies. Financial problems and rising living costs (including food and energy prices) affect shopping patterns. The cost of production may rise if energy becomes more expensive. If consumers become aware of the issues surrounding their products, they may demand that workers are paid a living wage, by influencing the law, or by choosing carefully where they shop. This, too, will make production cost more, and each fashion item will be slightly more expensive, as it has been in the past.

> *Customers want good value, but they care more than ever how food and clothing products are made.*
>
> Marks & Spencer, UK chief executive, Stuart Rose, 2006

The production and retail of the fashion industry makes a small group of people richer, and keeps poverty levels high in some countries. Fashion workers suffer from exhaustion and poor health, whereas consumers benefit from cheaper-than-ever prices.

Relocation, Relocation, Relocation

The relocation of production has created pockets of poverty around the world, where mills and factories have closed, causing job losses. Examples of this are textile mills in Northern England and garment factories in Toronto, Canada. Local production is better for the environment, as the clothes miles (the total miles an item is transported before being sold) are reduced, so less carbon dioxide is emitted into the atmosphere. However, because large-scale global production is cheaper, it now dominates the industry.

Controlling Trade

Free trade is trade that happens between countries without quotas or tariffs on imports and exports, and without subsidies. The price paid depends on the forces of a free market economy (see below). The international trade system is not entirely free, because tariffs, quotas, and subsidies control trade, especially between MDCs and LDCs. Some countries subsidize their cotton farmers by paying them yearly to continue to produce cotton. Rich countries use quotas to restrict the amount of foreign imports entering their country. This protects the industry in their own countries. The Multi-Fibre Arrangement (MFA) was a quota system that controlled imports of textiles and clothing into rich countries between 1974 and 2004. When it was lifted, China's strong and growing industry, previously restricted, dominated the fabric and wider fashion market, causing many other nations' industries to decline.

SPOTLIGHT

Free Market Economies

A free market economy is a trading situation where the price of goods or services is decided by consumer demand and global supply. For example, cotton and diamonds are both goods that are in high demand, but cotton is more easily available than diamonds are, which makes diamonds cost much more than cotton. Companies can influence the price of goods, too, by controlling or restricting the supply. This helps them to make more profit.

How Fame Fuels Demand

Celebrities and stars are extremely popular in many countries, and the glamorous global careers of women like Victoria Beckham, Sarah Jessica Parker, and Scarlett Johansson play an important part in the fashion industry. Designers provide free clothes to certain women, who act as an ad for that product in magazines, on TV, and when photographed in the streets. Because many women aspire to be like these stars, buying similar clothes is also very popular. Although *haute couture* (high fashion) clothing is too expensive for most people, an affordable version is usually mass-produced for the general public, so clothing companies are also dependent on these celebrities to sell clothes for them. Factory contracts can be created simply based on a celebrity's chosen outfit, but these contracts have very short deadlines. This forces factory employees to work overtime in order to keep their jobs and meet the MDCs' demand for celebrity style.

Celebrity stars such as Victoria Beckham and Katie Holmes, pictured here at an Armani event, play an important role in the global fashion industry.

> *Women are...scouring the web site to bag the latest celebrity trends. Shoppers can search [for clothes] by their favorite celebrity as well as by style. Its teen clientele can snap up a $75 lace dress inspired by one worn by actress Mischa Barton, or a $53 floral number à la Ms. Hilton.*

The Guardian (UK newspaper), writing about Asos.com, a fashion web site, 2008

Infrastructure

The global fashion industry, especially the export industry, has helped some countries in their development of infrastructure. Global trade routes need transportation, so there has been an improvement in roads and development of ports and airports to allow quick and efficient shipment of goods. The industry has contributed to urbanization, as factories have been built on what was previously agricultural land. These factories need reliable electrical power, so the power infrastructure of some countries has developed. Power stations have been built, and rivers dammed to generate hydro-electric power. In the countries where garments and accessories are retailed, shopping areas play an important part in town and city planning. As shopping has increased, more retail space is needed for global brands.

Population

The global fashion industry impacts on patterns and trends in population, too. In Latin America and Asia, for example, many people migrate toward urban areas and business districts that have factories. Labor exploitation in many factories has a negative impact on the health and standard of living of whole communities. In some cases, child labor is still used. The populations of MDCs are affected by the fashion industry as well. For instance, during the 1990s and first years of the twenty-first century, there has been a worrying obsession with dieting and other lifestyle choices, aimed at helping women to fit fashionable clothes and look similar to the models and celebrities who market them.

SPOTLIGHT

Bangladesh

The garment industry in Bangladesh is worth $10.5 million, employs 2 million workers, and makes up 68 percent of all exports from the country. Bangladesh's industry has been growing since the Multi-Fibre Arrangement (MFA) imposed quotas on some LDCs, but not Bangladesh. This meant that companies in Bangladesh, unlike those in China, could export as much as they produced. When the MFA quotas were lifted, China dominated but Bangladesh has continued to prosper despite this. Exports of clothing are now 22 percent of the country's overall GDP (total value of goods and services), and the average income has almost doubled in the last 20 years. However, many garment workers do not earn enough to feed their families—it seems that some people are getting very rich, while others are staying poor. In 2008, half of the country's population lived below the poverty line.

Retailers	Sales (2007–2008)	Profits (2007–2008)	Country where retailed	Country where produced	Monthly wages of workers	"Living wage"— enough to feed family and provide shelter	Conditions of workers in six Bangladeshi factories that produce for the three retailers
Asda (Walmart UK)	$31.9 billion		UK (Gross National Income: $2,608 billion)	Bangladesh (Gross National Income: $75 billion)	1,663–2,900 Taka (approx. $34–57)	5,333 Taka (approx. $115)	• Long hours (up to 80 hours a week) • Breaking labor laws • Forced overtime • Unpaid overtime • Verbal abuse • Physical abuse • Sexual harassment and abuse • No right to form a trade union • No contract • No maternity leave or sick leave
Tesco	$98.5 billion	$5.7 billion					
Primark	$3.6 billion	$444 million					

This table shows data on UK retailers and Bangladeshi workers from a report by the campaign group War on Want.

Indian garment workers near Rajasthan do embroidery work for Anokhi, a company that is renowned for its good labor conditions and investment in workers and their community.

Fashion and the Environment

All global industries have an environmental impact, but some impact more than others on humans and society. Below are some of the ways in which the growing global fashion industry is causing environmental problems, and impacting on human development.

SPOTLIGHT

Damaging Processes

- Producing maximum cotton yields means using chemicals and water on the farmland.
- Energy used in the manufacturing process, including the manufacture of synthetic materials (mainly from oil), causes gases to be emitted into the atmosphere.
- Each garment has "clothes miles" as it travels, often several times around the world, and this causes carbon dioxide to be released into the atmosphere.
- High consumption means high waste as many unwanted products are thrown away.

Impact on the Environment

- The gases emitted contribute to climate change.
- Factories contribute to global water shortages.
- Synthetic materials take a long time to dispose of and decompose.
- Habitats and wildlife are harmed by actions such as forest clearance and the use of fur in fashion.

Impact on People

- Growing cotton takes over cropland, creating food supply issues.
- Machinery has replaced some workers, causing job losses.
- The health and safety of workers is at risk, because of chemicals, fatigue, and other occupational hazards.

The Race to the Bottom

Large, powerful companies in the fashion industry compete with each other to deliver the best prices to their consumers. This results in a global race to find the cheapest sources of garments and materials, known as the "race to the bottom." Profit is a higher priority for many companies than checking that their garments and products are ethically produced, and there are many reports and news stories that demonstrate the poor working conditions and unfair pay in factories producing fashion items cheaply. For example, the campaign group, War on Want, produced the report *Fashion Victims* in 2005 and *Fashion Victims II* in 2007, highlighting the unfair working conditions and wages of workers producing clothes for Asda, Tesco, and Primark. One problem is that companies do not invest in factories but contract to local companies instead. These companies are known as "footloose multinationals." Local contractors have to compete by offering the lowest price, and workers do not have many choices.

University students in the UK campaign for a living wage for workers producing clothing for the clothing retailer Primark.

SPOTLIGHT

Sweatshops

Some workplaces in the fashion industry inflict poor conditions on workers. These include very long hours, very low wages, and a lack of rights for employees. Factories that ignore the law regarding employee rights, or are based in a country where there are few employment laws, are nicknamed "sweatshops." Organizations and charities campaign against sweatshops, by using media exposure. For example, a recent protest against the UK's Primark chain, organized by No Sweat, included five politicians, a celebrity, and the National Garment Workers Federation of Bangladesh. Campaigners criticized conditions and wages in factories where Primark clothes are made. Several TV programs have also criticized large clothing retailers recently in Western countries.

> *I can't feed my children three meals in a day with my earnings. This is my fate.*

Ifat, a Bangladeshi garment worker in the report
Fashion Victims II

Fashion and Identity

The reasons why we follow fashion are wide-ranging, and connected to our identities, or image, in society. There are "rules" for what is acceptable for different people—for instance, the "normal" dress of a teenager is different to that of someone in their thirties, or their sixties. A person's ethnic and socioeconomic background also influences what they are likely to wear. Fashions change depending on setting, too—for example, a person's work outfit and shoes are often different from their weekend clothes, but both could still be up-to-date, fashionable, and recently bought. Furthermore, clothing and accessories can represent our status, and in some cases, even show whether we are married. Fashion can advertise political beliefs, favorite music, religion, or cultural pride based on the color, style, fabric, and slogans on a T-shirt, suit, or shoes. Vibrant and colorful West African dress in global cities such as London, Sydney, and New York stands out and perhaps shows the wearers' pride in their culture.

Women shop for fashion accessories in Rajasthan India. Traditional styles of clothing such as the sari are still highly popular in many parts of India, but Western styles are also catching on.

> The pantsuit is [Hillary] Clinton's uniform... her wardrobe is a way of reminding voters that a woman can have as much bravado as the boy.
>
> *The Washington Post, 2007*

Fashion Freedoms

Unfortunately, people's fashion choices sometimes cause them to be treated negatively or unfairly. There are many cases where people are excluded because of what they wear. If someone cannot afford labeled clothing and shoes, this can lead to issues such as bullying and harassment, and even theft by the victim in order to "fit in." In several cases, of violent attacks on young people, clothing or footwear has been one of the issues raised in police reports and at trials.

> *They don't have to be like everybody else, but there is a great comfort to fitting in, there's a great comfort to feeling part of a peer group, part of a community.*
>
> Sarah Jessica Parker, BITTEN Clothing web site, 2008

No Two T-shirts Are the Same

Globalization is a complex process and there are many different sides to the global fashion industry. This industry impacts on our lives and our environment. Each fashion item consumed has a different route and story behind its production. In the case studies that follow, some of these routes and stories are explored.

For some young people, "gothic" fashion like this is a way to stand out from the crowd and get noticed.

Retail Fashion: Designed for All

The Australian department store, Myer, showcases its Spring/Summer Collection in 2008. Industry sales are increased through fashion shows and advertising.

The phrase "retail fashion" usually refers to fashion that is available at stores in shopping malls and downtown areas, providing affordable clothing to most people in society. These stores are easily accessible, and many of them have larger sections for female fashion, since sales in this sector are highest, despite a steady rise in men's fashion in the last few years. Retail stores and shopping centers are the traditional outlets for the fashion industry in MDCs, but supermarkets, out-of-town stores, and internet web sites are catching up. Sales online have steadily increased over the last few years, but unlike retail districts, most products are bought from Monday to Thursday (weekends are the busiest times for retail shopping).

Seasonal Styles

The fashion season has always been an important part of the industry. Traditionally, designers and retail stores changed their stock twice a year, for Spring/Summer and Autumn/Winter. Since shopping has become more popular, and production of clothes has become cheaper, customers can afford to buy many more items, so they go shopping more often, and the stores change their stock to appear new and exciting. Now fashion seasons are much shorter. This means that the whole production chain has to speed up, impacting on every person in that chain.

SPOTLIGHT

Fast Fashion

The trend for disposable, fast fashion has changed the global fashion industry. Retailers such as H&M from Sweden, Zara from Spain, and New Look from the UK provide quickly made, ever-changing stock. UK supermarkets, such as Tesco and Asda-Walmart, also change fashion stock quickly. Items usually take six weeks from design to point of sale, and are generally worn two or three times before being discarded when the next "season" of stock arrives. If a popular celebrity is seen wearing a designer outfit, fans can buy an affordable version within two months. This fast process means that factory workers may be forced to work overtime to meet the demand, because factories will lose work with the large companies if they do not deliver the products on time.

Chinese workers sew T-shirts at the Bo Tak garment factory in Dongguan city, southern China.

Information and Fashion

Media and fashion have an interdependent relationship. Media advertising creates a demand for fashion items, since consumers often find out about products through TV ads, magazines, and other media products. For example, the movies, *The Devil wears Prada*, *Sex and the City,* and *Confessions of a Shopaholic,* all promote shopping. Media also raises our awareness. News companies occasionally publish stories about sweatshops and poor labor conditions in the industry. Sometimes this can help improve situations, since companies have to respond to these accusations and investigate their own supply chain. However, they do not always know about every stage of the production chain—it is complex and a pair of jeans that were made in Tunisia may have buttons from another country, which does not appear on the label. Some people argue that it suits TNCs to remain ignorant, because managers do not have to correct poor working conditions if they do not know about them.

In the movie *The Devil Wears Prada*, Anne Hathaway plays a character working for a fashion magazine and trying to get to grips with the fashion industry.

Buying Your T-shirt

Every time you buy a T-shirt, your life is connected to farmers, factory workers, transportation workers who shipped it, and retail workers who sold it. This process might be different every time. You might be helping some people to achieve a better standard of living, and you might be supporting sweatshops and the prolonging of poverty without realizing it. There are ways in which you can affect the global T-shirt industry. You have consumer power and can choose which companies to buy from, based on your knowledge. You can use the internet to find out which companies support sweatshops. You also have power as a citizen (and soon as a voter) to make sure you are happy with the laws about cotton trade in your country.

Apparel workers in Rajasthan, India, cut fabric pieces which will then be sewn at another work station.

PERSPECTIVES FOR DEBATE

"Ten million cotton farming families in Africa are being forced into poverty because of unfair trade, which benefits just a few hundred cotton farming companies in the U.S.A."

Gael García Bernal on Oxfam International web site, 2009

"The answer is to... move forward with the free market principles that have delivered prosperity and hope to people all across the globe."

George W Bush, former U.S. president, speaking about free trade, 2008

Fashion Accessories: Big Business in Little Things

Sales in fashion accessories (including jewelry, handbags, belts, and hats) increase yearly. In 2007, they accounted for $1.9 billion in the UK, and an annual value of $20 billion is predicted in the United States by 2012. As in the garment industry, women's sales dominate, although men's accessory sales were still valued at around $3 billion in the United States in 2008. Women's handbags are the major seller, and ties and scarves are popular within men's sales.

Inexpensive Items

The accessories industry has experienced the same race to the bottom (see page 16) as other sectors, and as a result, people are able to consume more and spend less, because their products are made using cheap labor in LDCs. Although a financial downturn in 2008 has affected the whole fashion industry, some experts predict that accessories sales will increase over the next few years, as consumers buy scarves, ties, bags, and belts to update old outfits.

These handbags for sale on the street in Hong Kong are cheap imitations of top designs. "Fakes" like this are popular because they give the appearance of wealth without the expensive price tag.

SPOTLIGHT

Fast Figures on the Global Accessories Industry

- Handbags are the lead product in the industry in both the United States and the UK.
- Sales increased by 37 percent in the UK between 2003 and 2007.
- Sales of men's accessories grew by 31 percent in the United States between 2004 and 2008.
- The top four retailers in the UK accessories market are Marks & Spencer, Next, Claire's Accessories, and Accessorize (2006).

Handbags

Between 2000 and 2005, UK consumers spent $668 million on handbags. Instead of buying one good handbag, as many women have done in the past, consumers today can buy several, in different styles and colors. Designer handbags, some costing several thousand pounds, are popular, and many women associate these handbags with status: a stylish handbag made by Gucci or Chloe is another way to look and feel as rich, beautiful, and powerful as a celebrity. The trend for handbags is global, with fashionable women in Japan, Hong Kong, China, and India, as well as Western women, carrying expensive bags. It is a sign of wealth across the world, although some feminists believe that shopping, and especially buying decorative handbags that serve as accessories rather than functional items, holds women back and labels them as frivolous and concerned with beauty over more serious issues.

> Women's resistance to the pressure to shop has been around for decades, and feminists have long believed that an ideal world would be one in which: *Women would stop focusing on what they wore or the size of their bodies, stop spending hours and hours at beauty parlors. As for shopping! Only a ninny [fool] pursued such an empty-headed activity—a deliberate male chauvinist conspiracy to distract women from serious matters.*
>
> The Independent, Ireland, 2007

Jewelry Hazards

Jewelry sales also form a significant part of the accessories industry. However, many processes involved in jewelry production are dangerous, including gold, silver, and diamond mining. There are dangers for people working with less precious materials as well. The process of making popular or "costume" jewelry involves cutting, setting, and polishing stones, sometimes in cottage industries or at home, but often in factories. Many workers suffer from silicosis, a disease affecting the lungs, caused by fine dust from cutting and polishing minerals and gemstones. There are more than 500,000 sufferers in China, according to the World Health Organization (WHO).

Blood Diamonds

Diamonds are considered the ultimate rich fashion accessory. They symbolize the wealth of the wearer, as well as emotional ties such as engagement and marriage. But the global industry of diamonds is not as elegant and sparkling as the end products. In Sierra Leone, diamonds mined and sold by rebels funded a civil war that killed thousands of people and caused many children to be taken as soldiers. The rough diamonds found in streams and in the soil were sold illegally to smugglers, or exchanged directly for guns.

Miners search for diamonds among the gravel at the bottom of a stream in Sierra Leone. Their industry has been safer and more controlled since 2003 (see Spotlight opposite).

> *In America, it's bling bling. But out here it's bling bang.*
>
> Leonardo Di Caprio in *Blood Diamond* (2006), set in Sierra Leone

> *Diamonds are associated with positive events in people's lives, any association with anything violent is something that has to be addressed by our industry and has been addressed and will be addressed.*

Cecilia Gardner, World Diamond Council web site, 2009

SPOTLIGHT

Governing Trade

The Kimberley Process Certification Scheme is a legal process that has been in place since 2003 to control the movement of rough diamonds from mine to market. Some 74 countries worldwide have signed this agreement, stating that each stone must be accompanied by a certificate proving that it is not a conflict or "blood" diamond. The official agreement acknowledges that it needs the help of companies and governments also, to regulate the diamond trade effectively.

Diamonds and HIV

Diamonds have always been a precious resource, and mining has always been a risky job, where workers are exposed to diseases such as malaria, silicosis, and tuberculosis. Today, many people in diamond-mining areas in southern Africa have been infected with HIV, and there are frequent deaths from AIDS among miners. Mining areas are busy and overpopulated, with temporary and migrant workers, especially men, who are away from their wives and families. This has led to a large sex industry in these regions, and men may have sex with HIV-infected prostitutes and carry the disease back to their families. Debswana, a large diamond company owned by De Beers and the government of Botswana, launched an HIV/AIDS program in 2002. Employees and their families can attend education sessions given by their own community members, as well as receiving testing and treatment using antiretroviral drugs (ARVs), which are too expensive for many AIDS sufferers to afford otherwise. The program of treatment has increased the productivity of Debswana workers and reduced the amount of deaths, making it so successful that workers in De Beers' gold and diamond mines in South Africa and Namibia have also begun to receive support and treatment. De Beers has said that HIV/AIDS management is not only part of the corporate social responsibility, but also plays a key role in the productivity of the company.

Fashion Footwear: the Steps Made by Shoes

Many people spend a large amount of their wardrobe budget (and often money they don't have as well) on footwear, especially sneakers. For example, Americans bought 2.4 billion pairs of shoes in 2007, which is almost eight pairs per person in the United States. Nevertheless, the U.S.A. and European countries have mostly made a loss on the footwear industry over the last few years. This is largely because imports from the Far East, including China, Malaysia, and India, always undercut prices. This has especially increased since 2005, when quotas on footwear imports were lifted. Although there are many criticisms of labor conditions in LDCs, consumers still prefer the cheapest price.

Workers finish shoes at a factory in the one of the four largest shoe-making districts in China. Close to 20 percent of shoes sold within the European Union are produced in China.

SPOTLIGHT

High Heels and Health

The global footwear industry's sale of very high heels for women has impacts on health, according to experts. Women suffer injuries such as strains, harm to joints, and often get bruising, calluses, or bunions. One organization has estimated that the National Health Service in the UK spends $55 million a year treating foot injuries caused by high heels. However, the risks involved do not seem to deter most women from wearing high heels, and, like handbags, shoes are a product that women are generally prepared to spend more money on.

Shoe Repair and Waste

In the past, shoes were expensive, hardwearing, and difficult to find. Most people took their worn shoes to a cobbler to be repaired, rather than buy a new pair. Shoes were often black, to go with every outfit. Now they come in many colors. Vietnamese and Chinese-produced shoes are cheaper on the whole, and we buy more, so the design of women's shoes reflects this, adding details that make shoes appropriate only in certain settings. This means that you "need" more pairs. Waste is created when cheaply made shoes break, but also when high-quality shoes are thrown away because we stop liking them, rather than because of any flaw or damage. Most people in MDCs simply buy a replacement pair, though cobblers (shoe repairers) exist and are popular in LDCs, where secondhand shoes imported from MDCs are fixed and sold.

Vegans and Leather

Animal rights activists and vegetarians have created a demand for nonleather shoes. This growing market is largely made up of specialist shops and online companies selling quite plain footwear, although recently more stylish and fashionable shoes have been available for vegans and vegetarians. Natalie Portman, the actress who starred in three of the *Star Wars* films, has showcased a number of different vegan shoe designers, and for a little while, promoted her own line of high fashion shoes with the design company, Te Casan. Celebrity brands of fashion are very popular, since fans often buy the items that their favorite celebrity endorses, and recently, many celebrities have actually designed the footwear and clothing items that they promote.

The actress Natalie Portman attends the launch of her celebrity vegan shoe line, "Natalie Portman for Te Casan," in New York.

A man looks at sports shoes in the window of the Adidas flagship store in Beijing, China. Wearing sneakers is increasingly a reflection of style and fashion, rather than simply a practical choice.

Sneaker Technology

In the last 20 years, the popularity of sports shoes has grown considerably. Sneakers or gym shoes are now worn not only for sports, but also with jeans and other outfits, in many different situations. The sports shoe has diversified and met this demand. Technological developments in sports footwear have not only included air pockets for bounce, and materials that allow exercising feet to "breathe," but they have also included fashion features such as sewn patterns and large logos. Companies including Nike, Adidas, and Reebok spend millions on marketing shoes for sports and fashion wear, and celebrity soccer stars such as David Beckham and Cristiano Ronaldo front huge advertising campaigns.

> *Logos have grown so dominant that they have transformed the clothing on which they appear into empty carriers for the brands they represent.*
>
> Naomi Klein, 2000

The Anti-Nike Campaign

Nike is one of the most popular global brands in the world. Children in some U.S. schools mark their correct spellings not with a check mark, but with a swoosh, Nike's logo. Owning Nike sneakers is a dream of people all over the world. But Nike have received decades of criticism for poor factory conditions where their products are made, including accusations of child labor, pay below the cost of living, and intimidation of employees who want to form a union to protect their rights. According to *New Internationalist* magazine, it would take only 4 percent of Nike's marketing budget to pay every Indonesian worker a living wage.

Governing Alternative Trade

Fair trade in itself is becoming a sales feature, because it is more and more popular, but most consumers in this industry are anxious to know where their money goes and to feel connected to the producers. This requires more governance and control than the rest of the fashion industry. There are several ethical certification schemes, including national fair trade brands such as Fairtrade UK, and an international organization called IFAT—the World Fair Trade Organization. However, criticisms of fair trade are also common, and a new scheme is being developed, called the Sustainable Fair Trade Management System (SFTMS). This certification and governing policy should mean that producers who want to show that every stage of their supply chain is both ethical and sustainable can do so.

SPOTLIGHT

Ethical School Uniforms

In the UK, school uniforms are mass-produced for the cheapest price, which in the summer of 2008 was $12.50 from Marks and Spencer, $7.50 from Asda, and $6.69 from Tesco. The school uniform pack includes a shirt, skirt or pants, and a sweater or cardigan. But the same companies have been proven to use factories that pay their workers less than the minimum cost of living. Parents, schools, and schoolchildren may be unaware that their uniform policy and standards are fueling sweatshops and keeping the poorest countries poor. One organization in the UK, called Clean Slate Clothing, began developing organic cotton school uniforms free from pesticides that followed a fairer supply chain, to try to give parents the assurance that their children's uniforms did not involve sweatshops in their production.

> We have labor standards in our society. We have environmental standards in our society, but we let our companies go around the world to find the dirtiest and cheapest place to produce clothing to import back into our society, and we think that's fine. Children represent the hope of our society—we talk to them about ethics, but then we require them to wear school uniform that is produced like that.

Mark Rogers, founder of Clean Slate Clothing, 2008

Fair Trade

Most fair trade organizations express the belief that trade should do more than make profit at any cost—it should also fight poverty, address inequality, and help communities to develop. More than this, it should simply be fair, so that those involved get paid what they deserve for the work they have done, irrespective of what country they live in.

Beyond the Smiling Workers

Most of the information we receive about fair trade organizations is from those companies themselves. Web sites, leaflets, and even products show images of happy workers, making it difficult to be critical of such a movement. But many people still do debate the merits of fair trade fashion. Some common arguments are shown in the table opposite.

Workers knit gloves for the ethical retailer, People Tree, in Kathmandu, Nepal. The producer (KTS) provides education, training, and jobs for underprivileged people in Nepal.

Arguments For Fair Trade	Arguments Against Fair Trade
Fair trade not only allows workers to achieve basic standards of living, but certified fair trade organizations also pay a "community premium" for the development of the local area.	Fair trade organizations create inequality, because only those working for the company, living in a small surrounding area, can benefit, whereas whole areas of the world are in need.
Fair trade clothing and accessories are interesting, unique, and beautiful products that often reconnect their wearers with natural materials.	Because fair trade companies are usually small, quality control and other corporate systems are less effective, so products have faults or are poorly designed.
Many fair trade products are handmade, which keeps alive precious traditional skills all over the world, important to the cultural heritage of those places.	Continuing to support processes where clothing is made by hand actually hinders development, since machine processes could make more money for those communities.
Fair trade is becoming so popular that even major fashion retailers are developing fair trade clothing lines—it is considered good business sense.	Fair trade as one consumer choice among many will not change anything, it is still consumerism at the end of the day—in order to affect real change, you must examine the whole system of free trade, and use law and regulation to make trade fair. Also, the major retailers are competing with the small fair trade organizations and winning, but their methods are not as ethical.

The Future of Trade

The community premium is a sum of money that each fair trade producer receives on top of the fair price, to invest in local community and infrastructure. This is the strongest reason to support fair trade for many, and consumers are creating positive change and development through their buying patterns. They are helping one small community, though, not more. Trade rules, a lack of proper regulation, and demand for cheap, fast fashion regardless of human cost are huge issues that can only be touched by alternative fashion TNCs. Overall, too many TNCs in the fashion industry are currently involved in exploiting people at a global level, and it would take more significant change, and more widespread support of ethical and sustainable traders and producers, to affect this.

PERSPECTIVES FOR DEBATE

"How can a few extra pennies a day from fair trade be celebrated as an outstanding achievement for the poor?"

Steve Daley, WORLDwrite, 2007

"Fair trade doesn't just mean paying a fair price. It is an entirely different way of doing business, where the objective is not profit at any cost, but to help people in the world's most marginalized communities escape poverty and promote sustainability."

People Tree, Fair Trade clothing retailer, 2009

Becoming an Active Global Citizen

What is an active global citizen? It is someone who tries, in their own small way, to make the world a better place. To become an active global citizen, you will need to get involved in decisions that others make about your life and the lives of others around the world. Consider how the world could be changed, such as improving the environment and political or social conditions for others, and seek information about the issues from a variety of sources. Then go public by presenting your arguments to others, from classmates and local groups, to national politicians and global organizations.

In Your Life

It is easy to forget that we are all connected to the global fashion industry every day. Everything we wear has been made by a company to sell to consumers, either directly or indirectly. In order to engage with how fashion products are made, you could try the activities below.

1. Choose five items of clothing from your wardrobe, and see if you can find out what they are made from and where they come from.

2. Which is your favorite clothes store? Visit it and look at the labels (or talk to the store manager) to find out how many different countries the clothes are sourced from.

3. Global trade is said to spread peace and cultural exchange across the world, since it helps people to work together instead of fighting or not communicating. The global fashion industry plays a vital role in this.
• Based on what you have read in this book, how much "good" does the industry do? How could it do more?

4. Explore Eco Fashion World's web site at www.ecofashionworld.com and search their "Online Stores" for companies that deliver clothes to the USA and Canada. Decide:
• How easy is it to avoid fast fashion?
• How does the web site encourage you to think about the fashion industry?

5. Walmart is now the world's largest buyer of organic cotton. Research Walmart's lines of organic cotton clothes and household goods by going to: www.walmart.com
• How many different types of organic cotton lines can you find?
• Do you think it is worth buying organic products even if they are slightly more expensive than those made with less sustainably produced cotton?

6. Explore the world of secondhand clothes exporting at www.tranclo.com, a web site produced by one exporting company. Work through the information, and check out the links "Secondhand Clothing for Export" and "Remade Fashion."
• Have you ever worn secondhand clothes?
• Why do you think that secondhand clothes may have gone out of fashion in the USA?
• Would you wear remade clothes?